DANCING WITH THE FISH

Poems from a long and lucky life

By Roger Wooller

A little risqué, a little sad, a little epic, somewhat mad.

© 2023 The author Roger Vincent Wooller asserts copyright over all the poems in this booklet.

Cover photo by Walt Deas (personal communication)

Author: Wooller, Roger Vincent

ISBN: 978-0-9756368-0-0

TITLE: Dancing with the Fish

GENRE: Poetry, humour

PUBLISHER: Roger Vincent Wooller

Printed in Australia by Ingram Spark

CONTENTS

DANCING WITH THE FISH

Cover photo - A moment when a manta ray met a biology teacher, who should have known that fish are vulnerable to fungal skin infections caused by contact.

I met up with a manta ray to chat with man to man.

Mistakenly my manta ray was chatty as a clam.

He was a she and wouldn't speak. I asked her, "Will you dance?

She flicked me off and swam away without a second glance.

(She'd learnt the ranger's rules by heart,

She knew it was their wish,

That divers have to play their part,

*and **never** touch the fish.)*

1974 Heron Island

PANTIES

She wanted embroidered on pants, *and* her bra,
A message that told him that he'd gone, *too far*.
A motif that stated "If you can read this –
You're much too close, so give it a miss."

"Certainly Modom" the sales lady said,
"In what kind of script would you like it read?
Copperplate, San-serif, - Bold wouldn't fail."
She thought for a moment, and then she said -
"Braille."

1998

COW ON THE ROOF

*As a kid, reading Dr Doolittle books left me convinced that I could talk to animals. After the Brisbane River flood of 2011 a cow was left stranded on the roof of a house as the water went down. She had a **Yorkshire accent** and seemed disoriented. I couldn't resist a chat.*

I saw that cow up on the roof,

A chewin' on its cud.

I said, "How did you get up there?"

She said, **"There was a flood."**

"I know I'm really stuck up here,

I've never learnt to dive.

My head for heights has no delights,

I know I'll never thrive,

On corrugated iron

Nor scrapings from the gutter.

My dess-pair's reached its deepest depths

My pessimism's utter."

"Oh, never fear dear Cow" I said,

"I'll throw you up some jam and bread

And later, lots of grass and hay

So you'll be happy all the day."

"How can I thank you?" said the cow
"This corrugated iron

Is telling me to get out now -

It's very hot to lie on.

Just spread your arms and catch me

As I plummet through the air."

"Don't do that thing" I cried,

"To me it's so unfair.

A flying cow's undignified,

I'll go and get a chair."

Just then a passing 'copter came

And hooked her round the horns

The cow said **"Time to swing it babe,**

I'll sign the ree-lease forms."

And the last I saw of that old cow,

Was lofting in the sky.

Checking out the rooftops

 With a connoisseur's clear eye.

I never found out that cow's name,

Without her life won't be the same.

On dark nights sometimes looking up

At roof-line silhouettes,

I see a bunch of bovine shapes

Performing graceful pirouettes.

It's hard to know what's what, what's not.

She's started secret dancing class?

Is she now the cow that's hot?

And smokes, instead of chewing, grass?

I'd like to think she'll look me up

And tell me all her moos

But maybe.. she's forgotten me,

And gone off on a cruise...

2011

CEDAR CREEK

Precious times with toddlers.

Ahh, What days

they were!

Of wine and roses, curious noses.

What Daze we in,

on river rocks ,

What craze on skids, what fun with kids.

in sun, and dapple, smelly napple.

Wicker hampers, bubbling champers,

rippling rill, and laughter happle.

Chicken roast down gravy dribble

Bubbly giggle tickle ribble.

1977

You were so small.
I carried you in a pouch,
Close to my heart, close to my heart.
You made me laugh
With the sheer joy of a father's pride.

I carved you a propeller.
You laughed, exhilarated
In your harness by the mast,
While we sailed and it spun
Its way to foreign shores.
And a forgotten bedroom shelf.

Dusted off years later and
Given away to your school fete.
I bought it back.
The memories in its rough-hewn wood
More precious
Than I would have thought possible.

1991

THE NEUROSURGEONS LAMENT

*In 2001 it was reported that a Dr Stuart Meloy made an accidental
discovery while using electrical pulses to cancel back-pain signals
passing along the spinal cord. Patients stayed conscious to help guide the
surgeon's probe to the correct place.*
*By chance he hit the wrong nerve and what this patient said was; "Oh!!
Mmm. Aaah-aah-Aaaaa!! You're going to have to teach my husband to
do that."*
*His life after that discovery can only be imagined. It might have gone
something like this:*

I was putting probe electrodes in a lady's spinal cord
To give her some relief from lumbar twitches.
But when I turned the current on, she cried out "Oh my lord,
That feels just like the bulge in hubbie's britches."

"Could you turn the current up? Actually, quite a lot!"
And being mister nice guy, I concurred.
It was scientific interest that made me run her hot,
But then the scientific picture blurred.

For I could see commercial gain, an implant in the spine,
Controlled by signals from a small transmitter.
Would be a winner, what I need - a mega money mine.
I switched my patient off; she did look fitter.

She smiled a lot and in advance made thirty more
appointments.
But I had other fish to fry, I set up clinics on the fly
And men and women flooded in - I wasn't selling ointments,
No sir! I sold remote controls and sent them off to die-

-from pleasure that they'd never dreamed they ever could
achieve.
I took my wife to restaurant close at hand.
A diner AAAHED emphatickly. "My trademark I believe?"
Wife said, "I **Want** your one electron stand."

In nightclubs no more mobile phones lay littered on the tables,
Remote controls were clutched in clubbers hands.
And dancers mostly stood quite still, a gasping at the labels,
On bottles, deaf to music from the bands.

And when I used remote control to open garage door
The air was rent with groans from round the block,
The neighbours, **begging** me, for more, and more and more.
An **ee**-lectronic pastor, with my elect-**rec**static flock.

A flock in shock "Flock off" I yelled in burgeoning despair,
As they crossed their eyes and buckled at the knee,
Quite suddenly I'd realised that this wasn't very fair
'Cause nobody was left to.......implant............me!

2001

THE SCENT OF YOUR HAIR

Your first lock's smell is sweet and milky,
Powdered bums and sparsely silky
Fresh clean nappies, giggles coos.
Surprising eyes and sudden spews.
I sniff again, it's sun-bleached now.
Mostly clean, but sometimes sour,
Boisterous games with shouts and tumbles,
Bike barked shins and backyard rumbles.
Another sniff – there's oil and grease,
By day, but later comes release.
It's darker, combed and carefully gelled,
Smoke, beer, mates they all are smelled.
A sniff for luck –it's shampoo clean,
And bouncy like I've never seen.
Another smell is there just faint.
A pleasing smell of girl - "It ain't,"
You say, embarrassed. But one whiff
Shows kiss and kisser to my sniff.
Another sniff smells wedding cake,
Champagne and photos by the lake.
And later comes the smell of fear -
Mine, not yours, "Don't join up dear."

No locks to sniff for two long years
Then, with a note soon soaked in tears
Your lock of hair, cropped short and spiked,

With cordite smell...

"He was well liked."

2009

THE **S U O I E A X** OF LIFE

I was once a baby thug, my bum was wrapped in chux.

I drank my fill from mummy's dug and said "Mum this stuff SUX"

I grew up fast I was no fool. I searched around for rocks,

To make myself a fighting tool I put them in my SOX.

Drugs soon became the latest rage, I came to crave a fix,

It happened at a tender age, I think I'd just turned SIX.

Much later in their teenage years, my friends were walking wrecks.

I'd left the drug scene to my peers for I'd discovered SEX.

And now I'm into middle age what helps me to relax

Is music – now I'm so serene because I play the SAX.

1988

OLD TOM'S DAUGHTERS

Over a breakfast which stretched into lunch Old Tom told us of the troubles he'd had rearing his five teenage daughters after his wife had died. Tom, too has passed away, but his troubles live on.

Old Tom had five hardworking girls. He kept them on the run.
Molly mustered,
Tilly tallied,
From sparrow's fart they played their part they never had
much fun.
Hetty herded,
Pammie ploughed,
and Susan sighed for her love could die if her dad got out his
gun.

The lads wooed out from the outback town, to test their manly
pledge.
Willie wheelied,
Jimmy jumped,
Five girls were bait to quicken the gait an' stop any from
being a veg.
Charlie called,
Reggie revved,
and Simon sighed for his would-be bride in the house behind
the hedge.

"I'll stop you bastards" shouted Tom, "I'll pull that hedge of
broom."
Backhoe burrowed,
Grubber gouged,
"The gall of my girls for glowing their cheeks as red as my
roses in bloom."
Dumper delivered,
Roller re-levelled,
and the five girls cried, now no lads could hide near the
windows of their room.

Old Tom he thought he'd won the fight, to keep his girls safe
but,
Molly moped,
Tilly t'sked,
His life was hell and he could tell that of peace there wasn't a
glut.
Hetty howled,
Pammie pouted,
and Susan sat in a huff all day with the cat in the garden hut.

That night revenge! Lads chopped long branch, right off front
gate bush.
Charlie cut,
Reg retrieved,
They tiptoed up to Tom's bedroom, gave his window a bit of
a push.
Willie whispered,
Jimmy joked,
and Simon, leaning as far as he could, poked branch in
sleeping Tom's moosh.

While lads were laughing, Tom crept up behind, stole their axe giving lads consternation.
Reggie ran,
Willie went,
Whirling axe at their backs did a laxative thing, never again constipation.
Jimmy jellied,
Charlie crumpled,
and Simon sighted a notice next day, "FOUND, AXE. ask **at** police station."

But back the lads came with chainsaw again to give Tom a little more curry.
Willie whooped,
Jimmy jeered,
They tackled a tree - saw buzzed angrily, scattered leaves with hurricane flurry.
Charlie chipped,
Reggie ripped,
then Simon saw Tom bring out his shotgun. They departed in very great hurry.

"Tom's got us so beat we can't sleep we can't eat. Love's put us right off our grub."
Simon sickened,
Willie weakened,
"Anorexic dyslexic no-sex sick, but lovesick, tyres flat, our wheel's got no hub."
Charlie chundered,
Reggie regurgitated,
so Jim called a truce, they dressed up real spruce to meet old Tom down at the pub.

"We're real sorry" Jim said… "Hah - It's luck, yer not dead. Stay away from my girls you young punk."
Charlie chose,
Billy bought,
The beer flowed free Tom forgot the damn tree. Lads fueled this fine cause of their funk.
Simon sipped,
Reggie's round!
Old Tom accepted his grog from the boys, before they all knew, - he was drunk.

"You bastards are thinking you'll see the girls now, but my horse knows the way down the street."
Willie wisecracked,
Charlie chuckled,
They plied the old man with another anon - he had never had quite such a treat.
Reg raconteured,
Simon smiled,
and Jim lowered Tom's head for a post publial nap while the lads all got to their feet.

They led Tom's horse other side of the fence, to feed where the best grasses grew.
Reggie reccied,
Simon shushed,
Then they pushed Tom's sulky up close to the wire, poking the shafts right through.
Charlie chivvied,
Jimmie Gentled,
And Bill buckled the harness back on to the horse, the fence firmly between the two.

Tom woke, jumped aboard, spurred his horse, couldn't move.
The lads were long gone to their lass!
Simon snuggled,
Billy bedded,
Tom sleepily tottered his brain was distorted his horse he just
couldn't harass.
Jim jigajigged,
Reggie rogered,
Charlie cuddled. Safe in the sleep the old man would keep, till
dawn woke Tom up, in the grass.

By the time Tom got back it was settled and set, the boys had
made all of their bids.
Pammie perhapsed,
Hetty hugged,
Tom's daughters delirious, won round the old man, despite all
their didn'ts and dids.
Tilly twined,
Molly married,
Susan was satisfied, smugly she said, "Papa you'll soon have
Grandkids!"

And true to her word that hardworking bird, the Stork, started
filling the Cot.
Hetty huge'd,
Susan Caesarian'ed,
And Pam pointed out the potential to Tom. "Of workers you'll
soon have a lot!"
Tilly twinned,
Molly multiplied,
Tom was not such a git that he couldn't admit - "This is better
than what we had got!"

2012

So much to do, so little time in the hectic life of a young father, back in the days before throwaway cars.

Monday afternoon.
Love wife, love car. Home early from work. Check oil in car.
Surprise! Oil level higher than before.
Has engine found way of making oil out of thin air?
Thinks: Patent invention, put oil companies out of business, Get rich quick.
How can patent idea if not understanding?
Hmmm. Maybe petrol pump diaphragm is leaking petrol into engine oil…
More likely.
Oh well. Buy new diaphragm.
Try several shops.
No spare diaphragms anymore for $2. Can only buy whole pump for $100.
Down with motor manufacturers.
Grind teeth, retrieve old pump from similar engine at friend's place.
Getting late, but afternoon all planned out.
Daylight: Will replace petrol pump.
Dark: Will make new radio antenna. Then early bed.
Love wife.
Car not so popular.
Get home, change into dirty clothes, reach for spanners.
Not there.

In wife's car. Oh well. Change plans.
Make antenna first: Reach for tape measure. Not there.
In wife's car.
Wife not home yet.
Wife and car both unpopular. Oh well.
Get on with rust converting the trailer. Daylight precious.
Reach for squirt gun. It there. Good.
Vigorous pumping. No spray but acid leaks all over hand.
Oh well.
Use paint brush.

Wife arrive home on dark.
Hooray. Wife popular.
Get tools, remove pump, check diaphragm. It OK!
How can be? Oh well. Put replacement in anyway.
It late. I tired. But antenna must go up.

Reach for tape measure in wife's car. It not there. She
say,
"Look in drawer."
Have looked in drawer ten times but look anyway. It
there.
Wife unpopular again.
Vow to deck Designer of Destiny when I die.

Make up antenna. When ready it late.
Need wife hold fishing rod while I shoot line and arrow
over trees.
Idea is: tie line to rope, haul rope over tree, hoist antenna
into position.

Wife covertly hostile. Wants to go to bed.
"Silly idea fooling around this late."
I not popular.

I shoot, line snaps. Arrow disappears into suburbia with
fishhook, line, and sinker. Probably nails neighbour's cat.
Wife overtly hostile. Heads for bed muttering.
Get ladder. It clank loudly. Neighbour comes out to fight
burglar.
"Only me" I say.
"You brave" Neighbour say.
Wonder why. Think of spiders, snakes, push leaves out of
face, shiver.
He say. "Tree not strong enough for YOUR weight."
Agree. But darkness diminish sense of height. Increase
bravery.
Hoist antenna. Don't fall out of tree.
Neighbour retires disappointed.

Fall into bed. Wife still hostile.
She say, "Not tonight dear, diaphragm leaks."
I get headache. Confused.

Wonder if new diaphragm can be bought separately or
must whole unit be changed.

1982

HAGAR IN THE RED SEA

A precious moment on the foredeck while sailing to Spain with Jan on watch in the cockpit and our two young sons asleep below. At the north end of The Red Sea in winter, the wind builds to gale force from the Northeast, swings round to Northwest then dies away to calm. Suez is a long beat to windward.

I'm in awe.
Quiet pride as she shoulders aside
The great swell, in her ride, through the dark night.
*The wind is **strong** and it's rising.*

The foredeck dips downward, awash and a'sway,
The Nav-lights glow brief on the whip of the spray,
And the strain in the ropes makes the music they play,
While they're singing the song of wind rising

Let it last… let it last… *let **this** moment last,*
The song of the rigging, the pitch of the blast.
The dance through the stars of the top of the mast.
*Even though the wind's **stronger** and rising.*

I must turn to my task with halyard and winch,
Now to fight flapping mainsail, try not to flinch,
And reef, fold and tie it within half an inch,
*For I ken the wind's **roar** that it's rising.*

Exhaustion in motion, so hard to claw back,
Down swooping deck, to check on her track.
The sea is still violent, the night is still black,
But we're safe from the howl of wind rising.

Be still and ride gently, my gull on the swell
It will end, will this spell
Of wind Rising.

2019

IN OUR HOUSE

In **our** House We are **such** a posh lot!
We know how to live. Just look what we got.

The dog drinks out of the toilet bowl,
The geckos shit on the paintings.
The ants eat the soap in the shower,
And the scraps bin is busy fermenting.

Roots **tilt** all the pavers this way and that,
The termites have terrible manners.
With mouth full of house they continue to chat,
And the taps all need turning with spanners.

Like nappies the changing of light bulbs is due,
To dirt, from the flirting of insects with death.
And the stove top tries to pretend that it's new,
But it's missing a knob and it's near its last breath.

There's a vine likes to prise tendrils in through the boards
And we let it, - to see what's the next it will do.
In winter the mice like to visit like lords,
They nibble and choose from our larder what's new.

But we're posh,

Gosh we're posh, you can tell from our nosh.
We never eat straight from the floor.
Without cleaning it first with a hygienic wash,
We don't want you to think that we're poor!

2008

SAGA OF THE STRADDIE CROC

Since crocodiles have been protected by law, soaring populations and climate warming have driven them south of the tropics. One was sighted by kayakers on North Stradbroke Island in February 2023. Controversy raged among Islanders. A drone was sent up. It photographed a dugong. It didn't see the other thing that half the crowd on Bradbury's beach were pointing at, so the matter was never settled. Or maybe it was…

They saw a saw-backed sea creature,
T'was spotted by the shore,
Myora way and on its way,
To One Mile furthermore.

It made a swish, a swirl, a froth,
Its saw-back darker than a moth,
Some said it was a Crocogoth.

And folks who hadn't seen it grin,
Convinced it wouldn't do them in,
Despite kayaker's keen eyesight,
Declared it was a Crocoshite.

But round the mangrove trees it crept
And salty saw-back tears it wept.
Croco-tears, the kind of tears you never should believe,
When dinner plans, - its plans for you?
Such plans it likes to weave.

The saw-backed monster seen again, abaft of Bradbury Beach,
Drew crowds of gawking fearful folk, a'standing… - out of reach.
And those who saw it surface said, "I knew it all along,
The saw-backed thing is obviously, - a mighty Crocagong."

But those who saw the photo from

The drone, just had to smile.

For they could see quite clearly

That it was a Dugodile.

And others said, "*A searchlight crew,*

With gunshots in the night,

Gave crocosteaks to all who knew."

Insisting they were right.

"But that's illegal, not the law!

Our wildlife's sacrosanct."

"If they really did that deed,

They never should be thanked".

The argument goes on and on

For nobody's been bitten yet,

And if they are, the odds by far,

Could favour shark bite as the threat.

And never will mere words unfurl,

The mystery of the Crocoswirl.

2023

THE GRAMOPHONE

Back in 1950s Kenya, long play records were an expensive rarity. As children we loved and memorised all few of them...

Aunty Iris lived with us, so many years ago.
She brought her son our cousin Dave, who grew up as our Bro.
And when we'd finished playing hard, we'd lie round in exhaustion
Soaking up the tunes and songs from Mum and Dad's collection.

"Serenade" and "Mantovani's singing strings", "Romance"
Wove their daydream way around,
 Gave our youthful longings sound.
"The King and I" and "Oklahoma!" "Oliver" with Nance
We sang them on our boats and bikes,
And on our great adventure hikes,
And no one ever heard our likes,
Singing into phantom mikes between our puffs and pants.

And now my mum is eighty-five and Iris came to
stay,
We found that pile of records that had long been hid
away.
Excited and for old times sake I bought a
gramophone,
So we could hear them play again with Mum and Iris
home.

It didn't work out quite the way, at first, that I'd
foreseen.
We sat around and let the sounds,
From half a century do the rounds.
They conjured back such happy times, erased the
years between
Sweet poignance welled up every eye
We couldn't speak, we daren't try
Just looked, each at the other…wry,
And so again unplayed they lie, in darkness and
unseen.

2007

"I need word from you. Word is Borscht. Is very beautiful Russian soup."

My friend ask me "What
The hell do you say
When your brain's got a clot
And your mind's gone away?

How do you tell them
You now want to die
But you can't say the words
And your memory's a lie?"

I say

"You write your doctor in advance
Is called a Health Directive
It give your doctor half a chance.
To make your death effective.

Here mine is.

If I become a cabbage,
Unable to move,
Unable to think,
Unable to groove:

I don't want a life,
Enabled by tubing,
Ignobled by drugs,
Nobbled, unmoving.

I want to have meaning so,
Chop me in pieces,
Sauté in butter or
Fry me in greases.

I want to be added
To buttered mashed spud
With onion, and beetroot
The colour of blood.

I've lived all my life
As if I'd been scorched
But now I'm a cabbage...

Use me to make ....?"

2022

When I am gone
Remember this

You opened for me
The flower of love

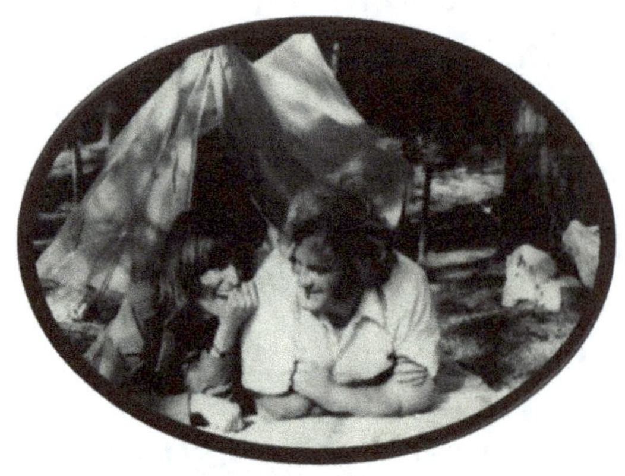

And because of you
I was not blind to the
treasures inside
And because of you
The flower grew and
fruited
And we ate together
that fruit
And planted the seeds
of love
Everywhere.

And now
In my ripening years
I look around and feel
Nothing but wonder
At how rich our life together
Has been.
I look around and see the sturdy seeds of love
Growing
And your Rogman is very content.

2014

www.ingramcontent.com/pod-product-compliance
Lightning Source LLC
Chambersburg PA
CBHW061104050726
47592CB00004B/1821